Live or Die

Certain names, dates and events have been changed to protect identities

Ten years from now where do you think you will be, me personally I don't know. I can't tell you where I'll be in 10 weeks let alone ten years. What I can say is this: live your life to the fullest and make the wisest decisions because with every choice you make there will always be a consequence. This story is based on real events, and I hope the things you read about today stick to your brain like a magnet to a refrigerator. You will read about betrayal, love and how one day your whole life can change so I strongly advise that you soak it up and take this book as a reality check.

Chapter 1:

The beginning

In a hospital unknown to me at a time unknown to me a set of twin brothers were born in Chicago, Illinois. They grew up loving each other with brotherly love and some would say the hardship they experienced inside their home, and outside their home made them so close. The Chicago area was full of violence and the street gangs left a massive impact on the Chicago area. Gang leaders were going to jail and gangs were dividing and going against each other. Big gangs such as "gangster disciples" "Black disciples", and "Black p. Stone nation" were the largest gangs in Chicago, and at one point they all had a mutual respect for each other despite them being opposite gangs. With the leaders in control things were bloody in the newspapers, but not as bad as it became when the leaders died or went to prison. It became a war in the streets disciple against disciple, gang against gang the crime rate rose to an all-time high and the Twin brothers, Malcom and Deion witnessed violence in their community daily. They witnessed so much violence from broad day robberies to fresh blood on the pavement, from shootings, that they became afraid to step off the stoop at their mother's house. Inside of their mother's home it wasn't safe neither with a violent stepfather they were in fear in home as much as out of home many nights they cried themselves to sleep. Their mother kept them in the house a lot because she knew how the world around them was. Deion wanted to play with his school friends and sometimes would cry because his mother wouldn't let him go outside. Malcom didn't mind after all; they had cousins who would come over routinely. Malcom looked forward to seeing his cousins whenever he could. One day Malcom was walking home from school alone while Deion stayed home because he was sick with the flu. A man near a trashcan began to light a crystal pipe hoping a piece of crack cocaine was in it but no smoke came out. Frustrated, he threw the crystal pipe and yelled “U DIE!” The man was a full blown junkie he had smoked a cigar full of PCP about an hour earlier and still wasn’t sober. Not knowing why the man was yelling and not smart enough to know a dope fiend when he sees one the 6 year old Malcom looked back at the man wondering what’s wrong and began to approach him. Malcom thought the man was homeless because he was wearing a ripped shirt, and the man’s pants were very dirty. Malcom said to the man (in one of the cutest kid voices you could ever imagine) “I can get you new clothes, my dad has a bunch of them, and here take my dollar it's my last one so spend it good.” The man’s eyes got huge, he snatched the dollar and then he snatched Malcom. The man’s face got intense with a mean mug on his face, so mean that Malcom had to close his eyes when looking at the man. Scared to death Malcom began shaking and then Malcom spoke, “Please.” The man’s hands were filled with filth he hadn’t showered in months, he then reached out and grabbed Malcom's mouth. The man said “Can’t help everyone HAHAHA,” The man laughed then he searched Malcom’s pockets, took his bag off his back and threw him to the ground. Crying loudly Malcom got up and ran home, when he got home he told his mother and stepfather what happened “MMOM a man just robbed me” he said. His mom with tears in her eyes said “It’s a cruel, wicked world that’s why I keep you in the house as much as I can.” “Did he have a gun or a knife?” his stepfather asked. “nneither” said Malcom shaking as he spoke. His stepfather laughed and said, “So how’d he rob you with his bare hands, SPEAK!” he shouted. Malcom began to tell them how he tried to help the man because he saw he was sad and homeless and Malcom’s mother told him in a kind sweet voice, “Son you cannot help certain people, you must stay away from people with evil faces they mean you no good.” Malcom’s stepfather began to think and think hard he did. He went into his room and began to sip some liquor he had in his cup from the night before, then he began to shoot a drug known as heroin in his arm. He took a belt, tied it around his arm and bit the long part of the belt hard with his teeth so he could tighten the belt. He then took the needle full of heroin and put it inside the tiny belt hole and pressed on the needle so the drug could go into his system. “yeahh” he said as he began to feel the high kick in. Loaded off of drugs and liquor he shouted, "You not a man until you kill COME HERE BOY” he then grabbed Malcom and made him come outside with him, then he said, “show him to me.” Malcom didn’t remember where the guy who robbed him was but he was scared out of his mind, so he began to walk to his school since he saw the man when he was coming from school.

Chapter 2: Murder

Deion was halfway asleep in his bed when he felt a presence over him, he turned around and saw his brother Malcom with a cold look on his face standing over him. The look on the 6 year old boy's face resembled the look of a grown man. Deion never saw his brother look like this before so he said, “yo, what’s wrong.” Malcom’s face was straight with no emotion and a tear fell down his face out of one eye, and he said, "I saw murder”. Then he laid down with his outside clothes on and shoes still on his feet and began to speak, “Daddy’s gone” he said. Deion was confused “where is he at?” Malcom got up and started crying as he began to explain what happened. Earlier that day Malcom and his stepfather went to find the one who took Malcom's belongings, and they found him. The man near the trashcan was full of pills and liquor and maybe a little bit of crack cocaine. While Malcom's stepdad was high off of heroin and drunk off of the liquor he consumed, he approached the man after Malcom pointed him out. The man near the trashcan was a pretty smart guy being on the streets for so long he understood things normal people didn't he was a crafty individual. He saw the boy he had snatched up and a man walking with him and that's all he needed to see, he began to say to himself "It's go time." He grabbed a knife he had and cuffed it up his sleeve, then he began to sit down and act like he didn't know what was going on. Malcom's stepfather while walking up to the man told Malcom "Stay here and watch a real man work and take notes." Malcom's stepfather walked up to the junkie, but before he could get close the junkie jumped up on top of the trashcan and started yelling "U DIEE!". Malcom's stepfather yelled "U FReak!" Then Malcom's stepfather pulled out a revolver, Malcom's stepfather was so high that he forgot to fully load the gun earlier and by it being a revolver he wouldn't be able to tell if the bullet was in the right chamber or not. Malcom's stepfather wasted no time and pulled the trigger, when Malcom's stepfather shot nothing came out and the junkie heard the click sound that the gun made from him pulling the trigger. The junkie started pounding his chest like he was a gorilla and said " YOu Tried to KILL ME Now you DIE!" The junkie jumped off of the trash can with the knife pointed at Malcom's Stepfather. Malcom's stepfather kept shooting the revolver hoping a bullet would come out (If he was sober he would've been smart enough to move out of the way). The junkie landed on top of Malcom's stepdad and the knife went in his chest, Malcom step dad yelled "U Freak!" Somehow Malcom's stepfather was still alive then a loud sound similar to a firework went off then another. It was the only 2 shots Malcom's stepfather had in the revolver; the junkie got up to run but dropped down dead halfway down the street. Malcom ran over to his stepfather to help him get up but he said to Malcom “Leave me NOw!” Malcom sat there and started crying and his stepfather said to him “Son in this life we live and we die my time is now, be a man”. Those were his last words; he bled to death on the spot and died. Malcom got up and started to shout as he cried hard and loud. He cried until he couldn’t cry anymore. He sat there next to his stepfather's body for about an hour, and even though gunshots were heard throughout the projects not a coroner arrived nor an officer, nor an ambulance. Malcom got up a changed boy on the inside and went home without saying a word. His mother was at work when the news hit. She had seen about her boyfriend's death on television, and she began crying and shouting "Why WHy me WHY!” while at work. She was fired on the spot. Her boss was a rich person who chased money so much that his heart turned cold. He was a person that would do anything behind closed doors for a higher position which equaled more power, and more money and living that way affected his sympathy. He almost had none so when he saw her crying on the job he was angry and felt like she was bad for business. She had worked there for the last ten years and getting fired, and losing her boyfriend broke her spirit so much that she turned to liquor as a result to deal with the pain. She became a drunk, drinking liquor almost all day every day and wasn't realizing the problems she was causing her 2 boys at home. One day Malcom and Deion's Grandmother came over and when she saw her daughter laid out in a bra and underwear with a bottle in her hand and a foul stench coming from her body, she told the boys to pack their bags and sent them to get in the car. Malcom's grandmother did some digging around her daughter's room and discovered a bag full of pills. When she saw them she held them in the air and turned to her daughter and said, "Jail or rehab" Her daughter stuck her middle finger up and her mother proceeded to call the cops telling her it was for her own good.

Chapter

3- Change

It had been 10 years since they'd seen their mother, and 10 years since Malcom witnessed a murder, yet the pictures of the blood and seeing his stepfather's eyes roll to the back of his head repeatedly flashed in his mind. Malcom at the age of 16 was suffering from PTSD and didn't know it. Deion and Malcom's grandmother lived in a rough neighborhood, and there were more kids in this neighborhood than the one the boys previously lived in. Deion loved being outside and Malcom followed behind him, the friends they had around them introduced them to drugs and liquor and now they were addicted to the substances.

The friends they had were the reason why they got into so much trouble, if one friend had a problem with someone the whole friend group had a problem with that person no matter the reason. Sometimes the boys would start problems just because it made them feel good and soon they began to grow in numbers from just 8 of them to more than 20 of them all clicked together in a group they considered themselves in a brotherhood. In order to hang around them on a daily basis you had to be someone that grew up with the boys or a relative of one of the boys. Deion and Malcom started hanging around the boys around the age of 7 so they were considered family to the boys fast forward 9 years and the love they all had for each other had grown tremendously. The boys committed their first robbery around the age of 13, one day they were all smoking and some drinking and saw a man who was dressed in fine clothes and had gold jewelry around his neck. There was a boy in the group by the name Devin everyone called him "Dev." Dev looked up and when he saw the man he said “Look.” All the friends, some couldn’t turn their heads fast enough, began to watch the man walk down the street admiring the jewelry he was wearing. “If we take that we’ll be rich it’s worth at least a million” Dev said. With their body’s full of liquor and marijuana they began to think crazy thoughts and together in under 5 minutes they came up with a plan. The man was a few blocks down the street, not wanting to miss out on an opportunity Dev and a boy by the name David ran first sprinting down the street Dev with a brick in his hand, Daniel with a stick. The rest of the boys followed behind them. Their plan was out of the window there was no time for a sneaky attack it became first come first served in their heads as they eagerly ran down the street hoping to take some jewelry home. The man looked back and saw Devin and Daniel running towards him. He looked closer and saw a gang of kids running behind them and looking carefully at their faces he knew these were some dangerous individuals. He pulled out a pistol and began shooting. When the kids heard the gunshots they began running back, “I’m HIT!!” someone yelled. That sent a wave of fear through the boys' bodies and some of them sobered up quickly. A friend by the name Antonio was the one hit. He ran to his aunt’s house she stayed nearby and she called for an ambulance when she saw the blood gushing out. “We almost had the money,” Dev said. “We almost died” Daniel said back. Dev became angry and rage ran through his veins when he heard Daniel say those words. Dev turned and said to all of the friends who were behind him “I’d rather take a risk and die a man, than live like a coward and die broke, Period” he said. Motivation began to spark inside the boys, and they began to plot on innocent people. They then began to realize that people who were innocent could call the cops on them and have them arrested but someone doing illegal activity would not call the cops, because people doing illegal things would need the police as far away from them as possible so they could succeed. Once the boys realized this, they began to look for weak drug dealers. They found success one day, while sitting on Dev's stoop they began studying the people's movements and daily routines around them. They saw a guy with a high yellow complexion around 100 pounds. The man looked weak and seemed like he got high off whatever it was he was selling. The boys after watching him for three days straight decided to attack, waiting for him to walk to a particular corner where he headed daily. The boys then jumped out on him and all of them together began to hit him. Dev for some reason always chose a brick as his weapon of choice and with the brick he went to work knocking the man out cold. They took his money and drugs and scattered. The profits they received weren't enough for them to all share equally, so they began to develop more of the first come first served mentally when robbing people and things got more dangerous as the days went on. Then soon they started to sell drugs getting drugs from their family members and robberies and soon became introduced to drug dealers that hung around their neighborhood who had large gangs and more money than the boys had ever seen. The big time local drug dealers would watch the boys as they moved in the streets and began flattering them giving them money and drugs and soon they would attach themselves to the boys more and more hanging around for a reason, not because they liked the boys. The drug dealers in the area thought that they could have the boys do their dirty work as far as robbing and killing if they could manipulate them or possibly pay them if it came down to it. Malcom was very smart and told his friends he saw through those guys and that one day they may be competition so they should stay away from them. Dev was all about a dollar and didn't care about what anyone had to say, in his head those guys were his friends since they looked out for him. He became blinded from the truth of the matter. Deion began to watch his brother Malcom's way of living and started to become concerned. Deion wanted to ask his brother to slow down on the drugs he was taking but he understood that he dealt with mental problems from things he had seen in the past so he let him be. Deion liked to party, if he wasn't partying he would drink a little liquor enough where he could feel the effect and still control himself, but when he partied he indulged in everything from hardcore pills, to marijuana and especially liquor. At parties he would get so drunk that he would blackout and his friends would have to carry him home or to the car most nights. Malcom took heavy drugs daily, he began to feel better when he was either high or drunk not knowing the effect they had on his health. One day while he was sitting on the edge of his bed with a gun in one hand and a bottle of clear liquor in the other, he began to feel a sharp pain in his chest. A few minutes later he dropped down to the ground and called out for help, his grandmother rushed in the room. Seeing him on the floor with a gun next to him she was shocked, "What's wrong?" she asked, trying to ignore the gun next to him so she could take care of her grandson. "I don't know" he replied. His grandmother called for an ambulance, before the ambulance arrived, she hid the gun in her room so Malcom wouldn't go to jail. He was suffering from heart failure due to the drugs he had consumed at a young age they had taken a toll on him. While Malcom laid in his hospital bed waiting to get discharged his brother Deion came into the room. "No more drugs" he said. Malcom looked the other way not saying a word, Deion tapped Malcom on the shoulder and said "Here it's Mom" handing him a phone. His mother spoke to him concerned, and you could hear her crying through the phone. Their mother was struggling financially, but not addicted to drugs and liquor anymore. She had relocated to Champaign Illinois, a town a lil over 100 miles from where the boys were. They all figured it was best if their grandmother raised them and their mother would pitch in when she could since their grandmother was doing better financially. Malcom rarely talked to his mother, so hearing her crying over the phone made him sad, but he showed no emotion, and he spoke to her with a calm voice. Once Malcom was discharged, he began to think about slowing down on drugs, and at the age of 16 was considering checking into a rehab. When he got back to his neighborhood everyone was happy to see him, speakers were blasting with music, and it felt like he had been released from jail after only being gone a couple of days. Malcom went to the house his friends referred to as the "kick it spot", which was one of his friend's cousin's home. That was the place the group of boys would meet up at, when Malcom entered the home there were girls all over the place "What happened" he said to his brother. "A lot changed in 2 days huh" Deion joked. The boy's popularity was through the roof and the females started hanging around daily attracted to their lifestyle. The boys would have fun by taking each other's girls and bragging about it with one another whenever they all would meet up. Deion didn't understand why they would do such a thing and started to question his friends' loyalty and would often then ask them about why they thought that was cool. They would laugh at Deion whenever Deion would bring the topic up, so Deion stopped speaking on it seeing his words had no effect.

Chapter 4

Respect

By the age of 18 Deion had earned a name for himself, whenever a problem would occur Deion would use his gun in a hurry. Whenever anyone inside of the friend group would get into a fight or a shootout, they would always share the story with one another, it was something they felt like they had to do to keep everyone updated on what was going on around them. Deion began to bring trouble to his friends that they weren't aware of because he wouldn't tell them certain things he would do. Deion developed the mind of a maniac, and things would turn for the worse in the year 1989. The boys would normally sell drugs out of one house together, but some of them began to spread out and would post up on street corners. A boy from the group by the name Fred was selling drugs on a corner next to an apartment complex. In the apartment complex there was another group of boys who sold drugs there, and they began to realize that they were losing customers. It was easy for Fred to take their customers; He wasn't doing it on purpose he was the first face the people would see so they automatically went to him instead of entering the complex. The group of boys came outside to see where their customers were going and then they saw Fred posted up outside of the complex with a hoodie on. They assumed he had a gun on him, so they all approached him. A few of the boys recognized Fred and told him to move around. “I’m getting money over here,” Fred said. This particular group didn’t have just young men, there were guys from the age of 16 to the age of 30 and the older guys didn’t take people stealing their customers lightly. “You heard what he said,” one of the older guys said to Fred. Then out of nowhere a teenager who was most likely out of his mind on drugs struck Fred in the face with his fist. Fred immediately pulled his gun out and began firing. Fred managed to hit a few of them but he was no match for the group, when the shots went off a few of them began to fire back. Fred was shot 9 times, “Stupid” one of the boys said, then he spat on Fred’s body and ran. Fred somehow survived and when word got back to his friends about what happened it made them all furious. They went to visit Fred in the hospital, luckily a lady spotted Fred bleeding on the ground and called an ambulance. Looking at his body, “It’s beef” Dev said, then he left the hospital. The group of boys wanted to retaliate and they did. “No small guns, only big guns,” one of the boys said. None of them had a car or a driver's license so they couldn’t get in a car with the guns, some of the guns were too big to walk on the street with someone might see them and call the cops. The boys had female friends, and girlfriends who had cars, so they began to persuade the women to let them use their cars. They told the girls they wanted to have a boy’s night out and that they were tired of seeing the same streets so the girls allowed them to use their cars. It was on, some tying shirts around their faces and some wearing bandanas on their faces and tying their hoodies down on their heads, began to get inside the cars with no plan of attack. The boys hadn't been in this situation before but knew what to do, they all got out of the cars and met up behind a building. Fred had given the boys a description of some of the guys, and he knew some of them by name. They knew enough but didn't know which building they were in. Deion had come up with a plan on the spot; he spotted a dope fiend (also known as a crackhead) and asked him where could he find some dope. The fiend pointed to a building, but Deion handed the fiend some money and told him to buy the dope from the individuals while he sat back and watched, also telling him he could keep it all for himself if he could keep his mouth shut. The fiend ready to get high, wasted no time and went in a hurry. When the apartment door opened Deion looked hard and said "Yea that's them, that's the spot come on". The boys marched across the parking lot gang deep, and looked like soldiers in the army the way they were crouched down with guns in hand. As soon as the fiend opened the screen door to walk out of the house and before the fiend could get out of the screen door fully Deion began aiming and yelling “RUN!” to the fiend. and he began firing. Once he fired everyone fired from Deion’s group and well over 100 shots were fired. The only one who had been struck by a bullet was the dealer who was coming to close the door, and his wound wasn’t life threatening because he managed to run up the stairs in time. Unaware that much damage wasn’t done when the boys got back they began to talk about what had just happened in a cheerful way, almost celebrating what just happened. Malcom was happy saying “That’s how you do it” over and over again. The boys watched the news hoping to see what they had just done appear. “Breaking news over 100 shots fired in the west field apartment complex and one person wounded, thankfully he’s not in critical condition and luckily no one died stay safe folks” the reporter announced.

The boys thought they'd hit multiple people but felt like they'd done their job by sending a message so they were pleased. Everyone was pleased with the outcome except for Deion. Deion felt like more people should have been shot or that someone should have died, and he began to express his frustration. "Leave it alone" his brother Malcom told him after seeing him talking to himself about how he felt. "If they come this way then what" Deion replied. The boys began to tell Deion that if trouble came they would handle it but they didn't feel the need to go back out there to kill anyone since their friend Fred was still alive. The boys decided to search for a party to go to since they still had the female's cars, and they found one. Inside the party Deion somehow got his hands on a few pills and began to get high and drunk so he could party harder. Him doing that made his mind run crazy with thoughts, and he put together a plan. Deion asked his friend for the keys to the vehicle so he could sit in the car because he needed some air. His friend told him "Just stand outside bro" because he felt like Deion didn't need to sit in a car in order to get air. "I gotta keep my back up against something, never let em catch you slippin" Deion replied. Deion's friend understood how he felt so he gave him the keys to the car. Deion grabbed a bottle of liquor he'd seen on a table and headed out the door. Once he was in the car he sped off and was spilling liquor as he drove because he hadn't grabbed the top to the bottle when he grabbed the liquor off the table. With liquor on his clothes and murder on his mind he began to drive to the apartments he and his friends had shot up earlier that day. He sat there and waited for someone to come out, then he said to himself "Somebody gotta die." He then walked out of the car and was so high that the apartment buildings began to look like skyscrapers to him. The group of men Deion were after had just been shot at earlier, so they were on guard constantly looking out the window. Deion didn't remember which door was theirs, just the area, and was walking around the complex with his pistol in one hand and a bottle of liquor in the other. Someone inside the apartment looked outside because they felt inside them something was wrong, and he saw Deion outside stumbling like a drunk with a pistol out and a bottle of liquor. "Man, who is this" he said to the rest of the guys inside the apartment. One of them started laughing and another noticed it was Deion, because Deion and his group were well known in the town. "He gotta Die" the boy who knew Deion said, because somehow rumors spread through the street and people knew Deion and his friends were the ones that shot up their apartment. The boy who knew Deion began to explain why he said that, and the boys ran outside quickly. Deion saw the door open because he was in the area and ironically, he was almost in front of the apartment door, the only thing separating him and the door was a field of grass. As soon as Deion saw the man opening the screen door he began to shoot because he knew it was one of them, then they began to shoot. Deion was outnumbered, so he ran behind an apartment building and they chased him. Deion was drunk and high and with it being dark he wasn't able to find the car. He ran behind a city dumpster and waited until he saw a body so he could dump the rest of the bullets in his clip. The boys came around the apartment building and were close to Deion, Deion yelled out "KiLL ME" and began shooting. As he shot they shot, and Deion was pulling the trigger so fast that his gun jammed, he managed to hit someone with 2 bullets. The person he hit dropped down to one knee and yelled out in pain, and that cry out is what saved Deion's life. When the boys saw their boy hit some of them went to get him up while the others still were shooting but from a distance. They stopped running towards Deion, had he not shot someone they would've chased him down and put bullets in him. Deion ran to the streets and ran into another apartment complex; he saw someone going into their apartment and asked the person could they unlock the laundry mat room for him so he could wash his clothes. The person was hesitant, because it was obvious Deion was high out of his mind and he had a strong stench of a liquor smell coming from his clothes. Deion continued to beg saying he lives with someone in the complex, and the person he lives with is at work or else he would get the key from them. The person agreed and once Deion was in the laundry mat room he got in a corner, took his hoodie off and placed it over his head and went to sleep. The next day Deion managed to find a pay phone; he had enough money in his pockets to call a taxi driver. Once he got back to his friend's house he tried to act like nothing happened, but the car his friend let him sit in was in enemy territory now, and Deion had to break the news and tell them why the car was where it was. Deion explained everything and his friends were angry with him but were still going to go with him to get the car back. The boys used to be able to walk through the city worry free, but now they had enemies and things wouldn't die down easily. Deion pulled more solo stunts, and in one incident he almost shot an innocent bystander, with the bullet grazing a young lady's arm in a shootout. After Deion found out he almost shot an innocent bystander he began to leave the solo stunts alone because he didn't want the wrong person to get hurt, Deion was a good man on the inside with a good heart. The beef was easy to dodge because the group of men they were after had so much beef with other gangs that Deion and his crew were only a threat whenever they ran into each other, they would rarely pop up to Deion and his groups neighborhood it was mostly Deion and his boys causing the problems, mainly Deion with his solo stunts.

Chapter 5

– Betrayal

"I got 500 dollars on it right now, I bet I can get her to take her clothes off," Dev said to one of his friends after seeing him walk a girl home. "I tell you what, let's date a girl and let's see who can get the draws first, I bet I get yo girl draws before you get mine and I will match yo 5 wit double, so let's make it a thousand since you gettin money," his friend replied. Malcom started laughing and said, "I got a hunnit bucks on Dev". Deion was the only person who didn't find what they were doing funny. Deion stood strong on loyalty and believed it was wrong for someone you considered a friend to want someone you were dating, but those were the games his friends played. One day Deion's loyalty would be put to the test. All of the boys still would hang out in one apartment together they called it the spot, or the kick it spot. This apartment belonged to Dev, and a friend named Mat. One day when Deion was over at the apartment one of his friends asked him to look out for his girl for him while he and some of the other friends went out in the streets to collect some money he was owed. Deion didn't understand why he would leave his girl with him instead of taking her home or with him, but he didn't question it and agreed to look after her for a little while. Deion got hungry and got up to make something to eat, "Do you want anything?" he asked. "I want you", the girl replied. Deion walked off quickly and tried to ignore what she had just said. He began to get nervous and tried to stay as far away from her as possible. He went into the living room and sat on the opposite couch, and he felt an unusual feeling, like a heat wave hitting the side of his face and when he looked it was her. She was staring deep into his eyes like she was stuck in a trance. "You good?" Deion asked. She didn't say anything, she just looked the other way, and in Deion's mind that was his cue to get the heck out of there. Deion stepped outside and didn't want to leave the apartment since he had given his friend his word, so he began to talk to himself. His friends had arrived and noticed Deion stressing, "what's wrong?" his friend asked. Deion explained his girlfriend's actions and his friends started laughing, "You should've took her to the room!" someone yelled. Embarrassed, his friend went inside and slapped the girl and began shouting at her. One of their friends started laughing and running in circles and began shouting "Oh noooo!". "You know how the game go she chose him," Dev said before he burst out laughing. The next day while the boys were at a local store standing outside selling drugs the cops came by, and they sat in a nearby parking lot and began to watch the boys. One of the boy's named Zack was not only selling crack cocaine, but he began using the substance as well. Zack's eyes were always bloodshot red, but he wore shades that were so dark that at nighttime he could hardly see out of them. Zack was not in his right state of mind, and when someone leaving the store had accidentally stepped on his shoe's he lost his mind. He took the cigar he was smoking out of his mouth and while it was still lit, he then grabbed the guy by the back of the braids. He then smashed the cigar into the guy's face and the guy began to yell out in pain as his skin began to burn. “Yo chill” Deion said, but Zack didn’t listen and the police who had been watching the whole thing, had already called for backup as they turned the sirens on and began going after the boys. “RuN!” yelled Dev as two cop cars began to speed down the street with their sirens on. Zack who was off of heavy drugs with an uzi stuffed in his sweatpants started to run but fell. “PIGS!” he yelled as he got up and did the unexpected. He took the uzi which had an extended clip holding 50 bullets and started shooting at the cop cars. He was so high that he wasn’t aware of his surroundings and didn’t see the cop cars coming from behind him. He heard the sirens though and when he turned around, he began shooting at them too. There were a lot of people outside and Zack was spraying bullets everywhere hitting stores, cars, and innocent bystanders as well. Zack ran behind the store, and as he ran around the corner he was hit twice, once in the shoulder and in the leg. Zack had a jacket on with inside pockets, inside the jacket he kept extra bullets and had one more clip left. He with one hand proceeded to change the clip while jogging with blood spilling out of his body as he ran. "I'm a G!." He yelled, and he began to hear an officer yell "Over here!" Didn't take a rocket scientist to realize that the cops were closing in on him. He quickly cut a corner and tried to come up with a plan. He then saw a city dumpster and jumped inside of it, while inside he threw big bags of garbage on top of him. While inside he dug in his pocket for some cocaine he had in his pocket and began to try and sniff what little was left. He was addicted to the drug, it had control over him and even with his life on the line he couldn't control it. The cops had seen garbage bags being moved around as if someone was in the dumpster, so they surrounded the dumpster. They then moved the bags and saw Zack with white powder over his face and they yelled out “Don’t move or we’ll shoot!” That was it for Zack he was taken to jail for possession of a deadly weapon, possession of drugs, and attempted murder. His friends saw it on the news and couldn’t believe it, some even cried thinking he was going to jail for life. While in the interrogation room Zack was offered a deal to lessen his sentence, if he gave up some names of local drug dealers he knew he could get a lesser sentence. He then went even further and told them he knew about murders that had happened in his area, and that it would be easy for them to fingerprint the suspects because he also know where they hung out and sold drugs. That was enough suspicion for them to issue a warrant for arrest, and everything Zack told the officers was correct. The information he gave them was about the enemies he had beef with, he refused to tell on his friends. Zack's sentence went from a 20-40 year sentence to a 3 year sentence which he would only have to serve half of. Word about what he did broke out on the streets as people began to get arrested. His friends didn't care that he had gotten people locked up because all of them were still free, and they had been friends for over 10 years so as long as he didn't harm any of them, they still had shown him the same kind of love as before. Deion didn't accept what he had done, he felt like it was dishonorable to get someone put in jail in order to get out of jail. He didn't mention how he felt though and somehow in 6 months Zack was back on the streets. Deion met a girl by the name Mary. Mary was a nice girl and Deion's first girlfriend in years, with his last girlfriend being in middle school. He fell in love with Mary and started spending more time with her; she helped keep him off the streets. Now Deion was 19 and in love, he began thinking about his future with Mary and talked to her about having kids someday. Deion started seeing his friends less but would still pop up occasionally. Mary had a car she would pick Deion up and would tell him not to bring his gun in the car because she was worried about getting pulled over. Deion sometimes would still bring it because he was still in fear for his life, he had shot people before and didn't want to fall victim. One day when him and Mary were at a restaurant out on a date a guy took a liking to Mary, and when Deion came back from the bathroom he saw the guy talking to Mary. He stood still where he was because he didn't want Mary to see him, and he watched them exchange words. He then walked up to Mary and asked, "Who's that?" She answered saying, "Some guy that must like me, relax, I'm not going anywhere" she said. Deion speed walked out of the restaurant and pulled his gun out on the guy in broad daylight and many people were around watching him (This is why we say no to drugs). He was still a little drunk from earlier and had taken a pill earlier that day so in the moment he wasn't thinking clearly, he was high out of his mind. Luckily Deion wasn't an idiot and didn't shoot the guy, but he did rob him for his belongings and then shouted, "Disrespect Me U DIE!" He then told the man that was his last pass and went back inside the restaurant. "RUN!" said his girlfriend. She told him the cops were called and he ran out of the restaurant and threw his gun in a nearby dumpster. He later found a pay phone and told his girlfriend what street he was on and she picked him up from the nearest bank. "Why didn't you tell me to get in the car, why'd you tell me to run?" He asked. She explained that if he had gotten in the car it would've been easier for the police to catch him because the description of the car would've been given to them. Her smartness made him love her more. A week later he decided to introduce her to his friends and show her how he lived on a daily basis. He knew the games his friends played when it came to each other's girls, so he made sure to keep his eyes on her. The next day she called him and said she wanted some space and that he wasn't the problem, she just had a lot going on and felt like their relationship was too much for her to handle at the moment. He was sad about it but he knew it was temporary so he was ok with it. The next day he came outside and as he was walking to the spot his friend by the name Jack came up to him. Jack hadn't met Mary yet and when he saw Deion he said "Mann where you been, it’s goin down at the spot.” When Deion heard the news he was ready to get there, he had just been feeling down since his girlfriend told him she wanted to break up for a little while and now he was feeling up. “Oh yeah.” he said, then began to speed walk up the street to the apartment. When he got to the stairs of the apartment his friends were lined up, and they all began laughing as soon as they saw him. “Oh my goodness, it's the lover boy,” Dev said when he saw Deion’s face. Malcom saw his brother and with a pint of liquor in one hand he took his other hand and put it on Deion’s shoulder and said to him, “There comes a day when a man feels like dying today’s ya day bruh,” then he burst out laughing and fell down. Deion was still confused but understood the joke was on him and as his hand touched the door knob his knees began to shake for some reason. He went into the back room and when he opened the door he saw his friend Fred and Mary in the bed together asleep. He felt sick, and after looking at them both he closed the door, and walked outside. Everyone was making jokes about him, but he didn't care anymore; he had too much liquor in his system and his mind was all over the place. The next day he saw Mary and she was over there again this time with the other females and he began to feel uncomfortable around her and began to avoid her by going opposite of wherever she was. He couldn't escape her; she was around his friend group almost daily, and Deion fell into a depression for a little while. Deion was sitting on the stairs thinking about his life when he looked up and saw Fred approaching him. His stomach turned inside out, but he knew he couldn't show any emotion. "What's good!" Fred yelled out to him like nothing had ever happened.

Deion stood up and shook his hand and conversated with him as if he wasn't hurt by what he had done. "Who can I trust!" He began to say to himself, spilling liquor from his cup as he yelled. His brother Malcom came and talked to him saying, "You gotta bounce back bruh you let this girl ruin you, you look like crap and starting to smell like it to bruh." Deion began to get himself back together as the days went on.

Chapter 6 - The LIE

Deion and Malcom's grandmother had gotten ill. She was diagnosed with lung cancer and had to tell the boys the news, but she didn't know how to tell them, she knew they would be devastated by the news. She waited until they came back home. She sat in the living room waiting, and then around 12 o'clock midnight the boys came in together. "Babies come here," she said. "I'll be 20 next week grandma" Deion replied. "I don't care if you're 30 you'll always be my baby" she said with a smile on her face. She told them the news and Malcom was angry and began asking her how long she had to live. "I haven't been given a death date, but I can die any day" she said. Malcom became very angry, and stormed off to his room and slammed the door behind him. Deion, who was drunk, fell on the couch and started crying like a toddler. That made his grandmother cry for a bit, and then she said, "Stay strong young king it'll be alright, we all die love me while I'm here." That made Deion cry even harder, and he ran outside. Deion was so drunk that he started running down the street and went to a nearby park and sat on the bench looking up at the stars he began to talk to himself. Deion fell asleep on the bench and when he woke up, he saw a man sleep on the ground next to him. Deion felt sorry for the man and gave him all of the money he had in his pockets which was well over a few hundred dollars. Deion went home and began to appreciate his family more; he had an uncle that lived in town that he hadn't heard from in years, so he called him. "What's up unc" he said, "What's good neph" his uncle replied. The two of them talked for a good 30 minutes and began to hang out more. His grandmother had already broken the news to the rest of the family and Deion and his brother were the last ones to find out. It had been a few days since Deion's grandmother announced that she had lung cancer, and Deion's 20th birthday was tomorrow. Deion told Malcom they should throw a party for their birthday; Malcom didn't want to have a party saying he was tired of the same old thing every year. That night before they went to sleep, they began to talk to each other about goals and Deion asked Malcom why he'd never dated a girl. Malcom had never had a girlfriend his whole 19 years of life and his reason was that he hadn't found the right one yet." I gotta get you a girl bro quick" Deion joked. "Why so she can do me like Mary did you" Malcom replied. That made Deion upset, and he stopped talking and when Malcom saw he stopped talking he stood up and said, "Once a punk always a punk." That made Deion angry, and his mind went blank, he jumped up and grabbed his brother's neck so hard you could see the veins in his forehead. Malcom didn't try to fight back and began to drop to the floor hoping Deion would let him go and he did. When Deion let him go he jumped and slammed him on the dresser "My Back!" Deion yelled out. Malcom laid down in bed, and when he was in bed Deion went into the kitchen and looked for a knife. He came back and stood in the doorway saying, "If you weren't my brother I'd kill you." When Malcom saw him he laughed and said, "Cain killed Abel, don't use being my brother as an excuse, come kill me." Malcom went into the living room and put the knife on the table. While in the living room on the couch he turned the TV on and fell asleep. When the boys woke up there were balloons everywhere. “Happy birthday chump” Deion’s uncle said to him while handing him two hundred dollars. When he went outside all of his friends were out there and someone handed him a bottle saying drink up, Deion felt like a king. The boys partied and surprisingly Malcom stayed sober, but Deion was so intoxicated that he had to be carried inside and while he was being carried, he saw his ex-girlfriend Mary in the crowd. He began yelling “Die, Die!” as he went into the house. Malcom began to reconsider hanging around his gang of friends so often, he started to avoid them. After not seeing him for a while they began to show up to his house to get him to come outside. While Malcom was on the couch playing his video game he was interrupted by a doorbell. It was a few of his friends. “Where you been?” Dev asked. “Laying low out of trouble” Malcom answered. The boys laughed, and they all talked for a while and then left, but as the days passed, they would repeatedly call Malcom’s house trying to get him to come outside. Deion was still doing the same old things, selling drugs and robbing people occasionally. He became a heavy drug addict and alcohol user and went back to his ways of violence. One night while he was walking home, he spotted a guy he had robbed. Deion thought the guy might try to harm him for payback for what he had done so he pulled his gun out as he was walking. The man saw Deion but didn't see his gun and started walking up to Deion. "AWW Yeah!" The man yelled out as he approached Deion. Deion with a bottle of booze in one hand and a gun in the other didn't hesitate and didn't say a word he began shooting at the guy. He hit the guy in the torso, and the guy fell down. Deion walked up to the guy and standing over him said, "Nighty, Night Punk" as he pulled the trigger. The gun jammed, and with no bullets coming out Deion became angry he grabbed the guy by the shirt and began hitting him with the gun. One of Deion's friends saw what was going on, and he ran over to grab Deion. Deion was angry and wanted to shoot the person who sold him the gun believing that the person who sold him the gun knew it might not work. His friends began to calm him down and when Malcom found out what happened he began to lecture him. “ I don’t take life lessons from drug dealers,” Deion told him. The next day the group of boys’ lives would change forever. Malcom was back outside with his friends everyday now, and they had a friend by the name Trent who lived a lifestyle similar to Malcom. Trent would never date females not because he was waiting on the right one, but because he felt it made people look weak and he was proud and thought of himself as a player. All of the boys were sitting in the apartment and Trent got up and said, “I got a girl in almost every complex in this town, I must be the man.” The boys began to laugh, and someone yelled out “We gotta watch you, one day a liar next day a thief!” Trent didn’t find what he said funny and threw some money on the ground and then he said, “I’m a go get one of my best looking girls if you can take her this money is yours.” The boys began to laugh again, and someone told him to pick his money up and put his money back in his pocket. "Naw I'm serious" he said then he stormed out the door. The truth was, he was lying he didn't have as many girls as he claimed to have. The truth was he had a hidden love for all of the women in his life, and he refused to date them because his pride was too high. He boasted about how many girls he had and would often talk down on those in committed relationships often calling them soft suckers, and all along he was in love with multiple women. He went to one of his female's house to bring her around his friends so he could prove his point. He had just left her house earlier, so her backdoor was still unlocked for him. When he got inside he headed to her room, and once he opened the door he couldn't believe what he had seen. It was her in the bed with another man. He went ballistic and ran over and punched the guy. The guy was much stronger than him, and the punch seemed to not faze him as he got up and slammed Trent on the ground. He then stomped Trent's face and body before bending over to punch him. The guy laid back down, tired from the beating he had just given Trent. Trent got up and shamefully left the house not saying a word. When Trent was walking back to the apartment all of his friends were outside hanging out Fred was the first one to notice Trent. Trent had a knot the size of a golf ball on his forehead and his skin complexion was light so the knot was red. “Somebody beat the snot out this Boy LOOK!” Fred yelled. The boys turned around and began to laugh so hard that their stomachs started to hurt. “Have mercy on his forehead,” said Deion. One more boy jokingly said, “Trent the pimp got his butt whipped.” This made Trent angry, Trent yelled out “They jumped me!” The boys all got serious. The boys had a strong love for each other and wouldn’t allow one of their own to be jumped. They knew they had to retaliate. “What happened?” Dev asked. Trent began making up lies, saying when he went inside the girl’s home he didn’t know that there were multiple people in there. He said that when he went in, he went straight to her room and something inside him told him to look inside the kitchen, but he didn't. He said that when he went inside the girl's room, there was a guy in there. He said that when he saw the guy he was going to just leave, but the guy jumped up and got in his face and started yelling, telling him to get out. "I take no disrespect," Trent said. He said that since the guy was talking crazy he punched him, he said that after he punched him they started fighting and in the middle of the brawl someone came from behind and grabbed him by his legs. "Next thing I knew I was in the air" Trent said. He said that after someone slammed him they began to stomp him out, and the only reason he still had his teeth was because he curled into a ball to protect himself, he told the boys. "If I had my pistol I would've shot em," he said. "Wait a minute you walking around these streets with no gun, what's wrong with you" Dev said. The truth was he had a gun on him, Trent was so angry when he'd seen the guy in bed with one of his females that he had forgotten about the gun. When the guy slammed him, his gun slid across the floor. “Are they still over there?” Dev asked. “Duh” replied Trent. “Let’s go then,” said Dev. As the boys gathered around to get ready and head over to the house, Malcom went up to Deion and told him to stay. He told Deion that if it got critical they would come grab him and that Deion was too violent he may lose his head and shoot someone. Deion was drunk as always so he agreed with his brother and said with his arms around his brother “For you my brother I’ll sit this one out, but if it gets ugly someone will DIE.” Dev thought that Trent’s story seemed odd because he knew Trent wouldn’t leave the house without his gun, but with that being the only reason for suspicion he didn’t question it. The boys stormed inside the house with Trent leading the way. Trent stormed into the room yelling “Get up!” to the guy. The guy saw a crowd behind Trent and sprung up. He punched Trent and as Trent was falling, he pushed him into his friends, and reached under his pillow for the gun he had gotten from his previous fight with Trent. Dev saw him reaching, and without hesitation shot his gun at him, he managed to strike him in the head. The guy dropped to his knees like an actor in a movie. He was dead, and the female in the room began screaming so loud Dev pointed his gun at her, and threatened to shoot her if she didn't shut up. All the boys ran out of the house, and they went straight to the spot. They knew the police may come for them so they took all of their drugs, and guns from their kick it spot and told Deion what happened and advised him to not go to the spot for a while because things were hot, and it might get raided.

Chapter 7- The Trial

The cops were on their trail now, because the girl who witnessed the murder had called them, and she told them everything she saw. The apartment all of their friends hung out at belonged to Dev, and Mat. Dev left the apartment and went to his cousin’s house, but Mat stayed. Trent thought since he didn't pull the trigger the police weren’t after him, and he headed back to the apartment. The thing was all of the boys sold drugs and people knew their apartment to be an easy place to get drugs. Trent was a money hungry type of guy, and Mat didn’t want to leave his home thinking the same way as Trent. Mat let Trent in and some of their friends' customers began to come to them for drugs since no one else was around. “Scared money don’t make no money” Trent said to Mat. “You right about that brother,” he replied. The two of them were making more money than they had ever seen. Their reign on top was short lived and a few days later the cops raided the home. The cops found Trent and Mat inside and began questioning them. They told Trent that since he was the ring leader he could be looking at 20 years to life. "I didn't kill anyone," he said. "Then tell us who did!" a detective replied. The police knew that Trent had lost a fight and told him that they had a pure motive, retaliation. Mat on the other hand believed he was innocent until they told him that he was an accomplice to murder, and also told him they would throw drug charges on him to equal his sentence to a possible 20 years to life. The detectives cut Trent a deal if he gave up the one who pulled the trigger he could be looking at 10-20 years instead of life. His eyes began to water and he agreed to the deal. He was scared and told them who pulled the trigger "That's all you gettin out of me" he said. Mat was informed by his attorney what was going on, and was advised to take a deal because it was looking ugly for him too. He refused at first then after giving it some thought he agreed. “I want a custom deal,” he said to the detectives. “It don’t work like that, you take what we give you or you rot in jail!” a detective told him. Another detective that was in the room saw an opportunity, “What do you have in mind?” he asked. He told them that he knew where the killer was hiding, and he said he wanted his drug charges dropped in exchange for the information. They told him that they would reduce his drug charges by 30 percent and if he didn’t agree then there would be no deal. They informed him that they had people out on the search for not only the killer but the rest of his friends, so pretty soon his information would be worthless. Scared that if he waited too long he would have to serve life in jail he squealed. He told the detectives where Dev was and that night they went and grabbed him. Dev's attorney had told him what charges he was facing, and he was also informed about his friends who were cooperating with the cops. The attorney told him if a deal came up he should take it, because he was the main guy they wanted. Dev told the detectives everything he knew; he told them why he and his friends went over there and he told them everyone who was with him. The girl knew most of the boys, and she had also told them the names of the boys she had known and since Dev's story was similar to hers, they believed him. The cops were on the hunt searching for everyone who was involved, and they found them one by one. When the police captured all of the boys, the detectives began hitting them with evidence, there was no need for questions because they had everything they needed. Each person who was apprehended decided to try and cut some sort of deal for less time since they knew that the jig was up, everyone but Malcom. Malcom's grandmother and brother Deion helped him get a lawyer, and Malcom refused to tell on his friends. When detectives offered him a slight deal which wasn't much less time because they had all the information they needed he began to yell, "Integrity!" and would pound his chest, and demand to speak to his lawyer. Deion was unaware all of his friends were telling on each other and he continued to send them money while they were in jail. The days went by, and Deion continued to grieve for his friends and helped them out in any way that he could. One day he received a call from his brother Malcom. Over the phone he could feel the tension and knew something was wrong, "Everything good?" he asked. He could hear the pain in his brother's voice as he said, “They all ratted man, all of em.” Deion couldn’t believe what he was hearing. And began to tell his brother not to jump the gun and accuse anyone of anything. “It’s all right here in black and white” he said. He had received his discovery report which contained all the evidence against him and how it was obtained. “Don’t trust anybody and stay away from these imposters,” Malcom said. Deion couldn’t believe it, the guys he was ready to lay down and die for gave his brother up in a hurry to be sentenced to years in prison. “The girl didn’t even know me,” he said. Malcom then explained how his so-called friends not only told them who he was and how he was involved, but also where he was hiding. Deion was crushed by the news. Months later when the trial came everyone, regardless of the information they had given received 8 years or more, and multiple people received 20-year sentences. Everyone except for Malcom, since he had a lawyer he had a better chance and since he hadn't told the police anything they didn't know what to believe when it came down to what he had done. The female hadn't mentioned his name much only when shown a picture of him, and when his friends told what the others did they also had to tell what they did as well. Malcom was sentenced to 5 years for being there when the crime was committed and the police couldn't prove that Malcom was aware of the situation since he told them he just went with the crowd and hadn't paid attention to what was going on. Malcom told them he normally walked with his friends daily and didn't listen too hard to what most of them were talking about because it was none of his business. Even though what he said wasn't the truth they couldn’t prove it to be a lie, and since he didn't tell them what he did like the others had to they had to go with it, and that 5-year sentence was the shortest sentence given during the trial.

Chapter 8 - Confidential

As time passed Deion had begun to think about his life and the betrayal committed by his friends hurt him deeply, and he fell back into a deep depression. Deion made a vow to himself one day while in his room sitting alone in the dark, he said to himself “I’ll never trust anyone again,” and he meant it. He decided to change his life around and put the gun’s down, but continued to sell drugs because it was the only way he knew how to make money. His grandmother had known her grandson was selling drugs and couldn't take it anymore. The jail sentence given to her grandson had made her scared and she called on her son's Derrick, and Justin which were Deion and Malcom's uncles for help. Derrick and Justin owned a heating, plumbing and electric company. They showed up to their mother's house and waited for Deion to come in. Once he came in he was drunk and Derrick told him "Sober up boy, tomorrow you start work." Deion laughed and said, "I work for me." Justin walked up to Deion, standing in his face he said, "As of tomorrow you work for us, and if you cause my mother to shed tears again, I'm a hurt ya." Deion's grandmother would often cry because she was worried about her grandson's safety especially after Malcom was arrested. "Just make sure yo kids straight" Deion told his uncle Justin. Without saying a word Justin picked Deion up and slammed him on the table. The table cracked, and when Deion was down with one hand on his back, and the other on his neck, Justin walked up to him and snatched him to his feet. Justin was built like a lumberjack, and he began to choke Deion. While choking Deion it seemed as if his feet were coming off of the ground and with his back up against the refrigerator he began scratching and swinging as that was all he could do. “Disrespect me or one of mine again!” Justin yelled, then he let Deion go. Deion dropped to the ground and started gasping for air, he couldn’t talk and could hardly breathe. The next day Justin and Derrick came to their mother’s house around 7 am, they grabbed big metal spoons from the kitchen, and pots and pans as they proceeded to Deion’s room. “Wake up!” yelled Derick. The brothers then banged on the pans and pots with the big spoons and that got Deion out of his sleep. Deion was halfway asleep but when he saw his uncle Justin, he woke up quickly. He knew that today would be his first day of work, so he went into the bathroom to wash his face and brush his teeth, then he got dressed and walked in the kitchen to get something to eat. “No time for that,” Derrick told him. Deion was angry but he didn’t want to fight any of his uncle’s again, so he kept his mouth shut. He went and sat in the car and once in the car they drove to a fast-food restaurant and got Deion something to eat. “Can’t let you work on an empty stomach” Derrick told his nephew. The job was a new experience and under his uncle’s tutelage Deion became a pro. He now was done selling drugs and had slowed down on the drugs and liquor. He finally was living a good life, no longer living in fear looking over his shoulders and no more putting himself at risk of going to prison. The days turned to months and the months to years. Deion was doing good and living a life he could never imagine, getting up early for work and coming home late at night. Fast forward 5 years and now Deion had his own apartment and had a new girlfriend by the name Kendra. Kendra was pregnant with Deion’s first child and Deion was happier than he’d ever been. Deion received a phone call, and the phone call was from his mother.

She had told him that his brother was being released from jail tomorrow, and that she would be in town at their grandmas for a few days to celebrate. Deion loved his brother so much that he began to cry when he heard the news. With a baby on the way, and his brother being released from jail Deion with a bottle of liquor in his hand, began to think to himself about where he would be if he hadn't changed his life around. He then threw the bottle of liquor into the street and as he watched the glass shatter as it hit the ground his eyes began to water. He told himself that from that day forward he would slow down on the drinking and quit the drugs. The next day when his brother was released from prison, he rode with his family to go pick him up. They arrived at the prison in multiple cars and when Malcom walked out of the prison and saw his mother and grandmother standing side by side he couldn't believe it, he began to cry. When they entered the car Deion handed his brother an envelope with 1,000 dollars in it, and a card letting his brother know how much he loved him. Deion and Malcom partied hard at their grandmother's house this time without friends, only family, and no drugs were involved. Malcom's uncles put him on board to the job they worked at and in three months Malcom had a car. After seeing Malcom in a car, Deion bought one for himself. Malcom's friends from elementary school were still in touch with Malcom, they would send him cash while he was in jail. Malcom's friends lived in a state called Indiana and told him about how much money they were making, they also told him that they could help him get things going out there if he decided to travel out that way and join them. Malcom was impressed with the numbers he heard and joined them. His friends were selling drugs, but the money they were making from drugs was three times the amount of money Malcom made from working at his job. Malcom drove out there and as the months went by he began to make so much money that he called back home and told Deion he should join him.

Deion was hesitant at first telling his brother he was done with illegal activity. His brother didn't press him to join him; after asking once and telling him how much he was making a week he didn't ask him again. Deion's baby was born around this time and even though Deion and his girlfriend were making together more than enough to provide for themselves and the baby, something inside him wanted more. The numbers kept ringing in his head. "5,000 dollars, all I need is 3" he started saying to himself one day while thinking about his brother's weekly pay from drug dealing. He left the bathroom and called his brother, and once his brother gave him the address to the location, he began to pack his bags. Deion was honest with his girlfriend and told her that he was leaving for a few months to deal drugs with his brother. She threatened to leave him at first, but then she accepted it. Once Deion arrived all of his old buddies from when he lived with his mother were there, and he was happy to see them. Malcom introduced him to the main supplier and Deion grabbed his brother and told him to step outside with him. “Remember what happened back home,” he said. “Trust no one.” Malcom began to laugh then he said. “Tell me something I don’t know.” Malcom had plans of leaving Indiana; he had made enough money to be good for the rest of the year. A few weeks later without telling Deion, Malcom left and headed back home to Chicago. Deion had found out he’d left as the days went on and he hadn’t seen his brother. At first, he was worried but after calling his grandmother's home one day she informed him that Deion had recently stopped by. Deion was angry for a while, but the money was rolling in fast, so he didn’t leave. He got an apartment for himself and was rarely seen by his friends, he felt like the town was odd and that he didn’t fit in. One day Deion decided to go to a local deli while leaving he accidentally bumped shoulders with a white guy. The guy's face turned bright red, and he told Deion “Watch where you goin ya boy.” Deion felt like the remark was racist and he became angry, he didn't do anything though and walked off without saying a word. Deion started routinely going to Chicago to visit his family but resided in Indiana. His birthday was a few weeks away and he began to call his uncles saying he wanted a party back home. He had told his friends in Indiana about his plans of having his party in Chicago. They began to try to convince him to have it in Indiana. "Party wit ya boy" His friend Leon told him. Leon and Deion were close friends. Deion thought about it, but told him, "I gotta go back home and celebrate this one wit the fam you welcome to come." Leon, with a smile on his face agreed to come. Deion the next day decided to drive to chicago, he was going to his family something he did routinely. While in Chicago he began to contemplate going back to Indiana. When the day came for him to go back, he had a feeling inside his spirit. That feeling he felt on the inside would always pop up right before something bad would happen. The only time that feeling would rise inside of him is when a shootout was about to take place, so he hadn't felt that feeling in a long time. He went with his gut and stayed in Chicago another week, and then it happened. He had gotten a call when he answered he heard, "This is a collect call." When he heard this his heart started to pound as he accepted the call. It was Leon and over the phone he started to say "They got us man, they got us!" Deion was scared now, because he had drugs stashed in his apartment in Indiana. He thought someone might tell where his stash was for a lesser sentence. "How'd they get you?" Deion asked. Leon told them that when he went to give someone some drugs, that person turned out to be a confidential informant. A confidential informant is someone who is hired by the police to buy drugs from criminals and turn them over to the cops. The police had been watching them for multiple months and decided to send in the confidential informants a few weeks before Deion left for Chicago. The officers had been sending multiple confidential informants, and not only did they lock up each individual that sold them drugs, but they also had enough evidence to raid a few of Deion's friends' houses, and a place a lot of them sold drugs out of together. Deion couldn't believe what he was hearing, and he jumped in his car and got on the highway. He knew it may be a matter of time before he was next, so he went to his apartment so he could take all of the drugs out. He had almost 100,000 dollars' worth of drugs there and he began to flush them all down the toilet. He shed tears as he flushed because in his mind this was it, it's all over.

Made in the USA
Monee, IL
19 July 2025

21069182R00048